I0817365

First published in the
United States of America, 2019

Gingko Press Inc.
2332 Fourth Street
Suite E, Berkeley, CA 94710, USA
www.gingkopress.com
ISBN 978-1-58423-700-6

Published under license from Graffito Books Ltd
www.graffitobooks.com

Printed in China

Kit & Willy's Guide to.... Buildings

definitely NOT by Zebedee Helm

Gingko Press

the Introduction

Hello,
I'm Kit and this is my sausage-shaped deputy, Willy. We are FULL of something that my parents call CURIOSITY, which means that we like putting our NOSES into things and having a good SNIFF about (unless it's KALE, or the WASHING UP which we leave well alone).

In this book we are putting our noses (along with the rest of us) into BUILDINGS. Buildings are EXTREMELY useful things (you're probably in one right now). Without them we'd only ever be OUTSIDE, which is fine if it's sunny, but not so great when it's POURING with rain and your UMBRELLA got shredded on a research expedition.

What you will need

To investigate buildings **PROPERLY**, along with a holster full of pencils and a **NOTEBOOK**, you will need **LOVELY MANNERS**. These come in handy when dealing with the people you will meet at the buildings you're researching and who will hopefully be answering your **DIFFICULT** questions.

To discover **EVERYTHING** about some of the most interesting buildings in the world **PLEASE** turn the page, **THANK YOU**...

the PYRAMIDS (GIZA, EGYPT)

There is a lot of exciting **MYSTERY** surrounding the building of the pyramids but after **EXTENSIVE** research we can reveal that beyond **ANY** doubt they were built simply **AGES** ago by super strong Egyptian **GIANTS** with the help of **ALIENS** (in flying saucers getting the lines all straight). When they were finished, dead Pharaohs were popped in them with all their favourite treasures, which then got stolen by **ROBBERS**.

What you Will need

Rolls and rolls of **LOO PAPER**. When visiting the pyramids, if you wind yourself up in loo paper from head to toe (or paw), you will become an authentic and historically accurate **MUMMY**. This should provide **GREAT** entertainment to the other tourists **AND** keep you cool in the hot desert sun.

the GREAT WALL of CHina

(中国)

You can DEFINITELY see the moon from the Great Wall of China

goes on and on

nice roof

Longest building in the World (13,000 miles long)

Chinese kite stuck in tree

Like most walls, this was built to keep some people IN and to keep other people OUT, and as China is a very big country it had to be REALLY long. In fact it is the LONGEST building in the world, and would be EVEN longer if several farmers hadn't removed extensive bits of it to build their farmhouses with. Willy says it is the ONLY man-made thing on earth that is visible from the MOON, but sadly, like a lot of his favourite facts, this isn't actually true.

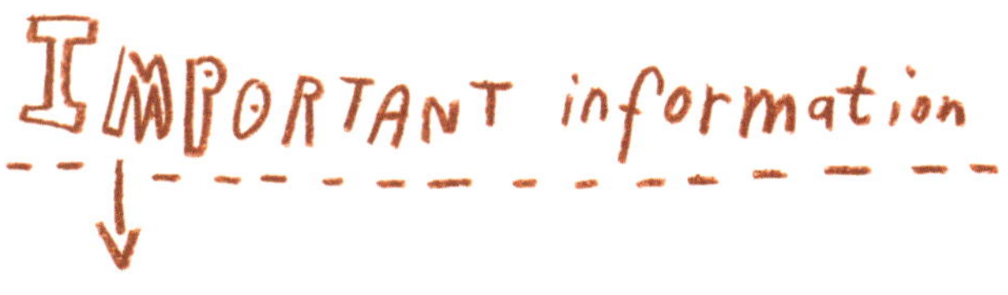

The bricks in the Great Wall of China are held together using STICKY RICE (that has been mixed with other top secret ingredients). If you are thinking of building a rocket to visit the moon, then DON'T use sticky rice, sticky TAPE will be far more EFFECTIVE at holding it together when you leave the earth's atmosphere.

the PANTHEON

(ROME, ITALY)

The Pantheon was built almost 2,000 years ago, as a temple to the Roman Gods, and it STILL hasn't fallen down! This is REMARKABLE considering the whole roof dome is made out of ANCIENT ROMAN CONCRETE. The building hasn't got ANY windows, so if you get bored of admiring it, it's perfect for kicking a ball against... but maybe actually you shouldn't, as these days it is used as a Church, and besides, it's SO old, that if you kick it too hard it MIGHT fall down.

What you Will Need

SOAP! The Pantheon has a LARGE HOLE right in the middle of the dome, which lets the light pour in, and sometimes also the RAIN. With its lovely ancient MARBLE floor, it makes the PERFECT shower.

NOTRE DAME

(PARIS, FRANCE)

This enormous cathedral looks impressive from a distance, but close up it gets **EVEN** better because it is **COVERED** in statues and **GARGOYLES**. The gargoyles' job is to spit the rain clear of the roof but the most famous one, **LE STRYGE**, just stares at Paris all day and looks completely **BORED**. At one point in history Notre Dame got **SO SHABBY** it was going to be knocked down. Luckily someone clever wrote a book about a **HUNCHBACK** called Quasimodo who lived in the towers, which reminded everyone of how **GLORIOUS** their building was, and they saved it.

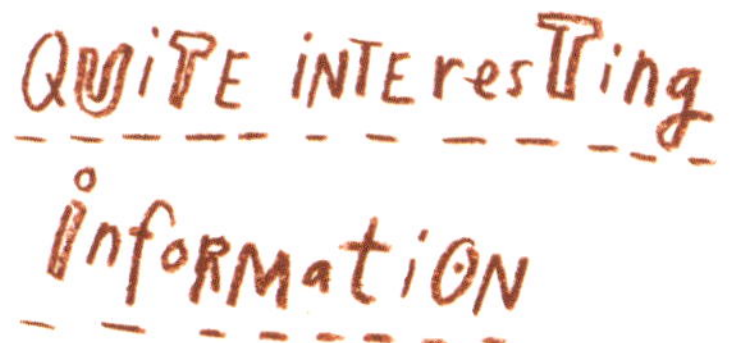

Notre Dame is rather grey on the outside but when it was new (800 years ago) the **WHOLE** building was completely covered in **BRIGHTLY COLOURED** paint. Annoyingly, the endless drizzly rain has washed it all off.

St. Basil's Cathedral

(Moscow, Russia)

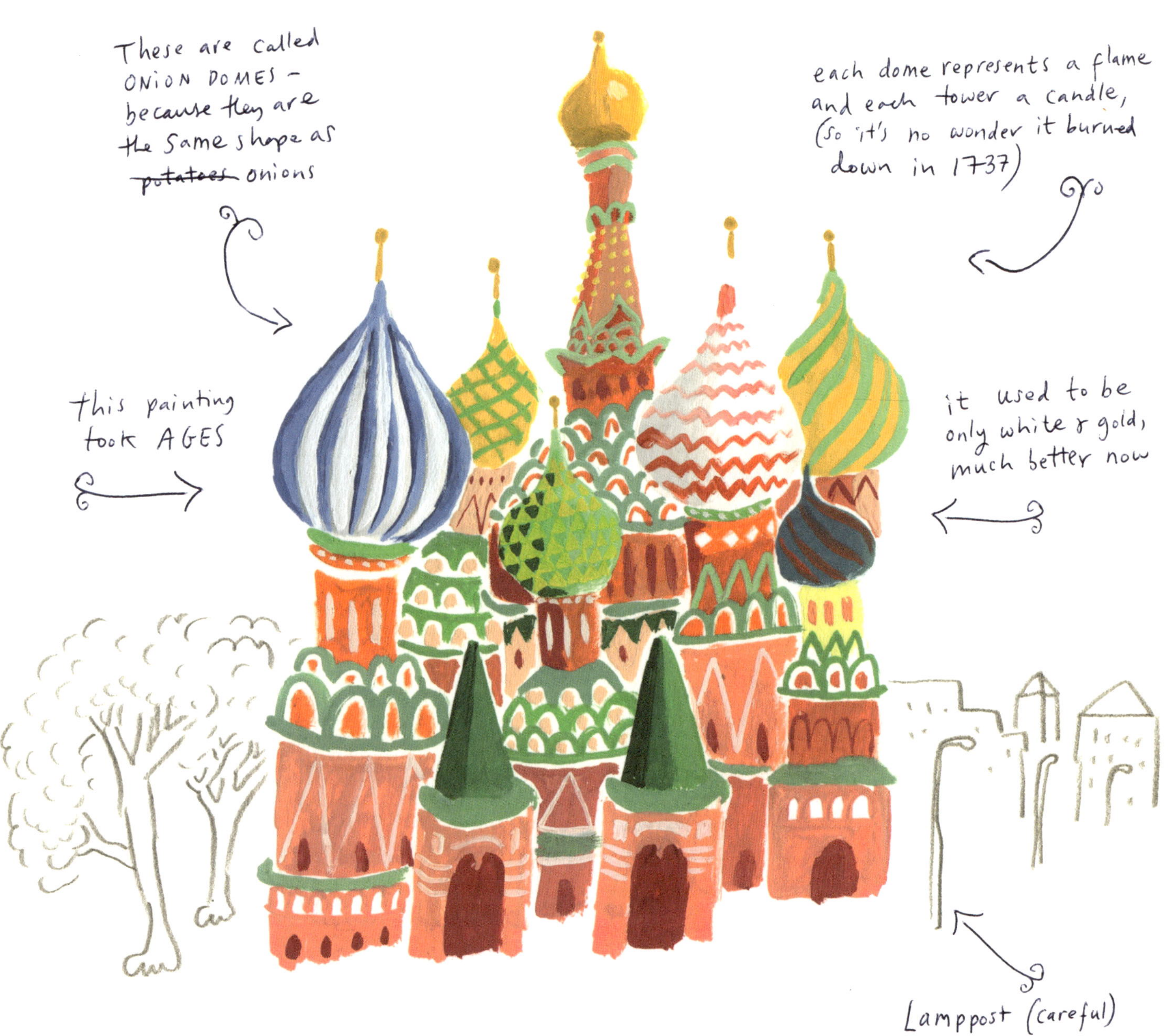

You'd be forgiven for thinking that this is a FAIRGROUND ride or a MASSIVE lollipop shop. Sadly, it isn't – it's a cathedral, and a museum. It was built by a man who went by the cheery name of Ivan the TERRIBLE, and he dedicated it to his best friend, Basil (who was really nice). These days the Russians MARCH past it during their military parades to show the world that they are MIGHTY and TOUGH but have a SILLY and COLOURFUL side too.

IMPortant ADVice

If you go to Moscow in the winter then DON'T lick a lamppost by mistake. They get SO cold that your tongue will STICK to it and you'll be GLUED there until the spring, when the ice melts and you can go back home.

the Taj Mahal

(Agra, India)

POLLUTION, oh dear

These are called MINARETS - They lean outwards on purpose, so if they fall over they DON'T land on the main bit

Lovely reflection

1,000 elephants helped build the Taj Mahal

400 years ago, when Shah Jahan's wife Mumtaz died giving birth to their 14th child, he was STRICKEN with sadness and decided to honour her by building the TAJ MAHAL and burying her in it. It changes colour during the day to reflect her moods: pink in the morning (sleepy mood), white at midday (hungry mood) and golden in the evening (party mood). Sadly now, due to pollution, the whole thing has turned GREEN and is starting to crack, and everyone is TERRIBLY worried about it.

Important Information

Pollution is an ENORMOUS problem so you should WALK everywhere, DON'T litter, and say NO to plastic straws.

NEUSHWANSTEIN CASTLE

(HOHENSCHWANGAU, GERMANY)

Try Spelling this! Gee!

and THIS!

Chitty Chitty Bang Bang was filmed here

pointy turrets

lovely views and vistas

River

Pine trees (handy for Christmas)

This is the ULTIMATE fairytale castle. SO much so that it was the model Walt Disney used for Cinderella and his fun parks. It was designed and paid for by MAD KING LUDWIG, who was shy and wanted to hide from the world in romantic SPLENDOUR. He loved the latest tech, and it was built 150 years ago, using STEAM - POWERED cranes. It was the FIRST castle to have central heating, running hot water and, in the garden, a RAINBOW - MAKING machine!

If you are going to build a fairytale castle, don't make it TOO complicated. Poor Mad King Ludwig spent SO long and SO much money building his that he only got to sleep there for 11 nights before he was ARRESTED for debt and taken away FOREVER.

TOWER BRIDGE

(LONDON, UK)

Tower Bridge is a useful bridge helping people get from one side of London to the other. HOWEVER it has a REMARKABLE trick up its sleeve. It can OPEN up to let ships sail through! It does this about 3 times a day and all the road traffic has to stop... but NOT ALWAYS. In 1952 a London bus was in the middle of crossing the bridge when it started opening. Instead of stopping, the driver speeded up and the bus JUMPED the gap!

A lot of people think that Tower Bridge is called London Bridge. Willy likes the story of the American billionaire who bought LONDON Bridge, had it shipped to the USA and once it was rebuilt, discovered his mistake! Sadly this is another Willy fact that isn't actually true.

good phone reception

Mr Eiffel had a secret apartment up here, with a GRAND PIANO in it.

Restaurant where Mr Maupassant had his lunch

There is an ice rink here in the winter.

Taller than the clouds

good lawn for picnics...

...apart from

The Eiffel Tower Was designed by ~~Mr Eiffel~~ Mr Koechlin, but Mr **EIFFEL** was in charge of the organising, so he organised the credit... for himself. When it was finished many Parisians hated it. A famous author named Mr Maupassant disliked it SO much that he had lunch in the restaurant there **EVERY** day, saying it was the only place in Paris where he could be and not have to **LOOK** at it! (The real reason was that the foodwas **DELICIOUS**).

What you WiLL Need

A PICNIC. Sightseeing makes you **VERY** hungry. You can buy ingredients from the market and make your own extra **LONG** French sandwich and then **GOOD LUCK** trying to choose a bun from a pâtisserie for dessert.

a French sandwich

the CHRYSLER BUILDING

(NEW YORK CITY, USA)

the secret spike

all this top bit is shiny steel

built by a motoring mogul but it isn't on wheels, it's fixed to the ground

Dentist up here

MASSIVE steel eagles for scaring the pigeons

a scared pigeon

arrgh!

down in the lobby is the world's FIRST digital clock

When this skyscraper was built there was a two - horse race in New York to see who could construct the tallest building. The other tower **THOUGHT** it had won, but while their builders were celebrating, the Chrysler Building builders sneaked an **ENORMOUS** spike out through the top of theirs, which added another **185** feet of height and the honour of being the tallest building in the **WORLD**. Annoyingly, it was beaten less than a year later by a third horse, the Empire State ~~Horse~~ Building.

The **BAD** news is that you are **NOT** allowed to go inside the Chrysler building to have a good sniff around as a **TOURIST**. The **GOOD** news is that the very toppermost of all the offices contains a **DENTIST** - so if you happen to have terrible toothache when in New York...

the GUGGENHEIM MUSEUM (NEW YORK CITY, USA)

nice view of it if you live here

GUGGENHEIM MUSEUM

front garden

Someone travelling in style (probably a famous artist!)

This was built to house Mr Solomon R. Guggenheim's art collection, which was really getting TOO BIG for his bedroom. Some people, rather rudely, said this building looked like an indigestible hot cross bun, but it's more like a SPIRALIZED plant pot. Inside it is one very long curvy corridor. The architect, Frank Lloyd Wright, hoped the public would go round it on MOTORISED chairs, listening to classical music by Chopin and Bach. Quite surprisingly this VERY good idea never happened.

That's terrible

But at least it's CURVED Mr Guggenheim, and it's yours for five bucks!

Solomon R. Guggenheim

TOP Secret INFormation

When the Guggenheim opened, the artists of the day were worried because they thought that, as the walls were CURVED, their paintings would all have to be curved too! Artists can be SO silly.

the SYDNEY OPERA HOUSE (SYDNEY, AUSTRALIA)

rare Australian cloud

pointy shell-like roofs – VERY good for ACOUSTICS (makes sounds sound LOVELY)

Boring buildings

person fishing (for sharks)

pretty reflections

This building VERY nearly didn't get built at all. There was a competition for its design and one of the judges (who didn't like any of the drawings he'd be given to look at) found this one CRUMPLED up in the BIN. It took 10 years longer to build than it was supposed to and it cost over a THOUSAND per cent more than expected, but everyone agrees that it was worth it. There isn't a MORE pointy, shell - like place for singing or acting, ANYWHERE in the world!

The architect came up with the idea for the design when he was peeling an orange, so if YOU think while PEELING FRUIT, you never know, you might have an INCREDIBLE brainwave.

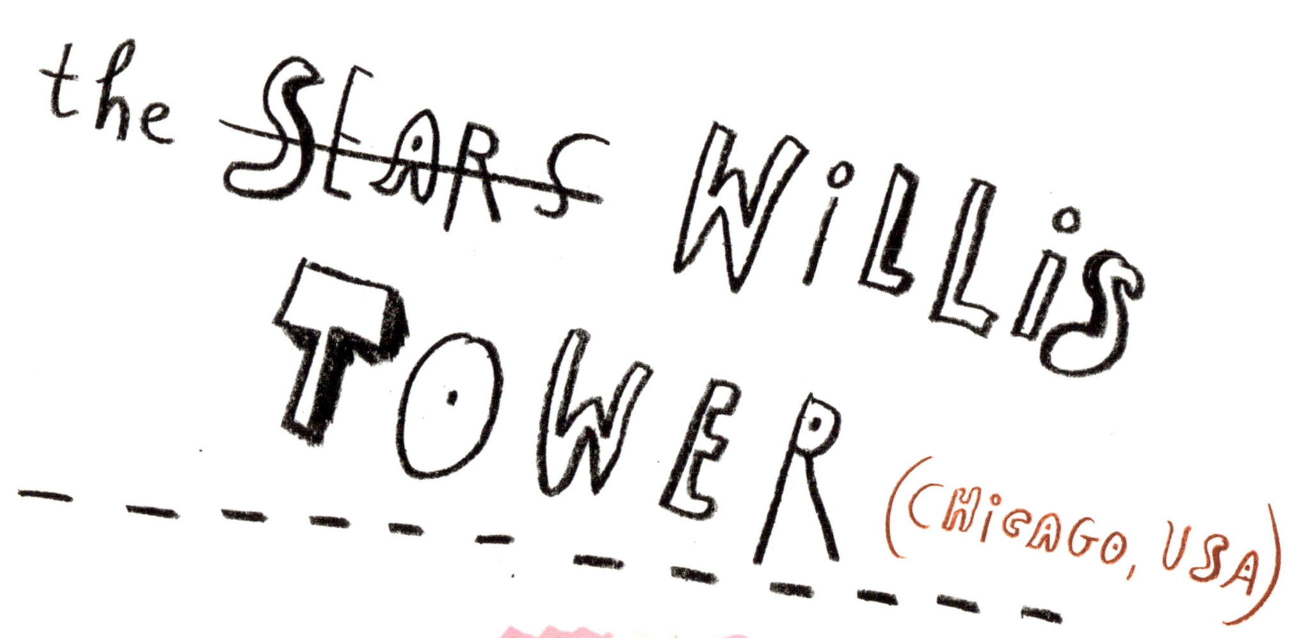

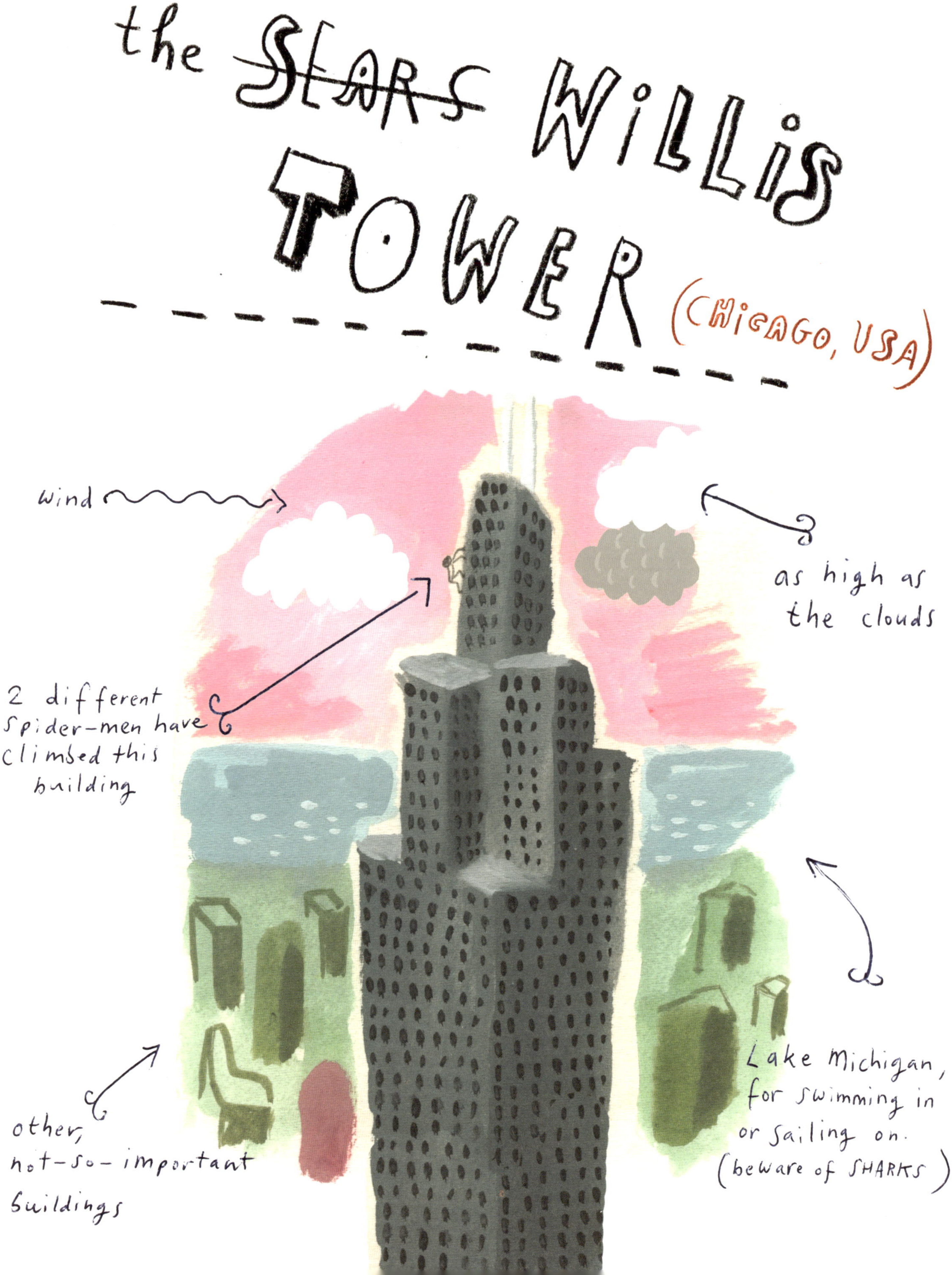
the ~~SEARS~~ WILLIS TOWER
(CHICAGO, USA)
wind
as high as the clouds
2 different Spider-men have climbed this building
other, not-so-important buildings
Lake Michigan, for swimming in or sailing on. (beware of SHARKS)

This skyscraper used to be the **TALLEST** building in the **WHOLE WORLD**. The only problem is that it was built in Chicago, which is one of the **WINDIEST** cities in the whole world. So on a windy day when you stand near the top of it, you can feel the whole thing swaying about. This is a **MAJOR PROBLEM** if you're trying to balance a spoon on your nose in the cafe.

This building has changed its name. For many years it was called the **SEARS TOWER**, and **A LOT** of people don't like its new name and will pretend they don't know **WHAT** you're talking about when you ask them (politely) for directions to it.

DAD-BUILT TREEHOUSE
(In the Garden)
unimpressed bird
good view into next doors garden
Rope Ladder (too short)
discarded hammer
Chair to reach the ladder from

Unless your Dad is a builder or a carpenter, or BOTH, the chances are your treehouse will be completely PRECARIOUS and not REMOTELY safe. But DON'T PANIC, as this is actually what you WANT from a treehouse. It makes being in it MUCH more exciting.

What you WILL NEED

A mature-ish Dad (or equivalent), a not-quite-suitable tree, random bits of non-matching timber, and then bandages, crutches and really good insurance for when the INEVITABLE happens.

the EndRoduction

There are MANY incredible buildings in the world - this is just a small selection - but in the same way that an elevator gets to the top of a building and can't go on any further because it's run out of building, we have run out of book.

What WE have LEARnt

Buildings are DEFINITELY a lot more than just shelters from the rain. But the BEST building of all, despite it (probably) not having any towers or hunchbacks or rainbow - making machines in it, is the one YOU live in, the one you call HOME.